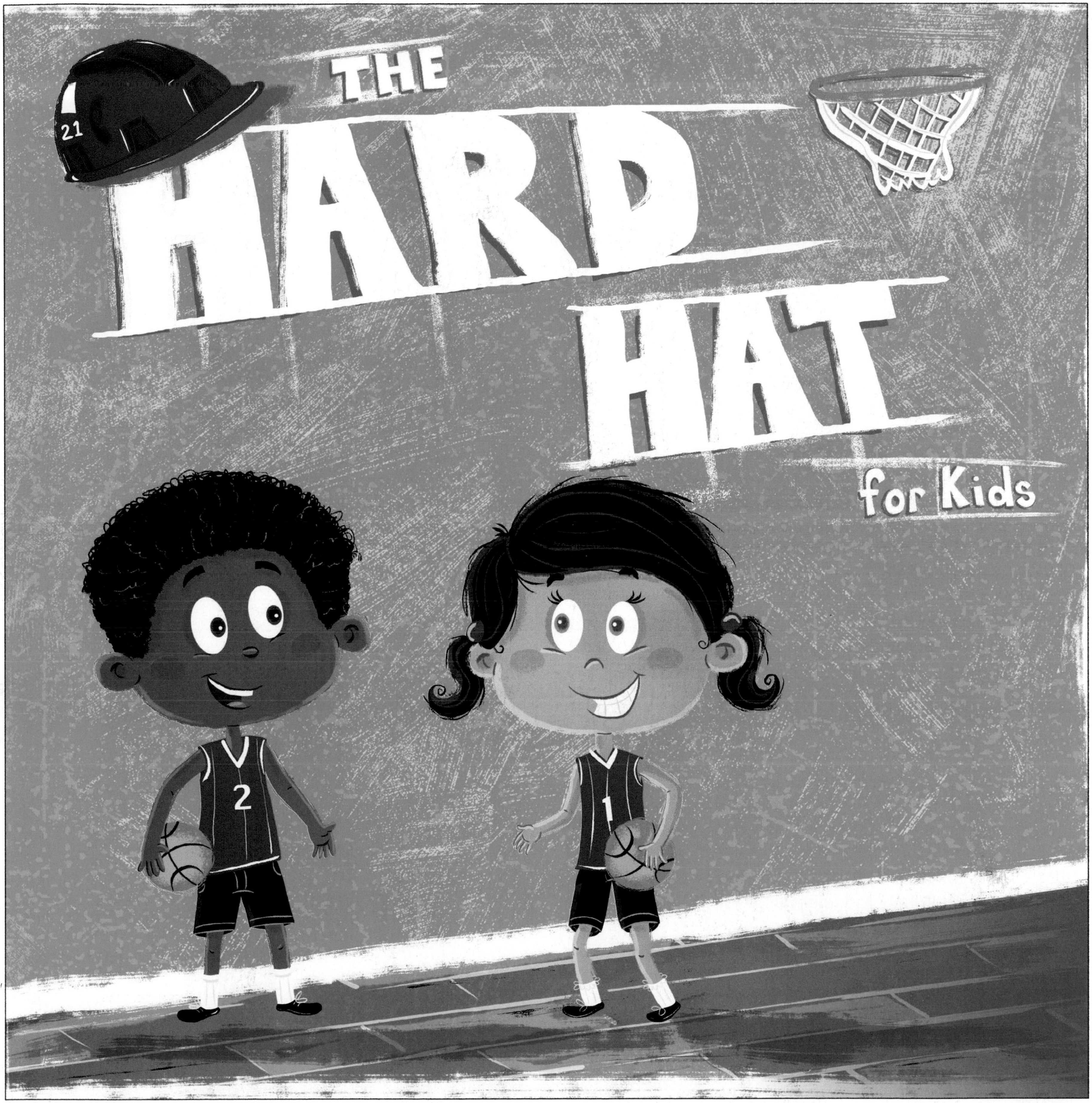
THE
HARD
HAT
for Kids
21
2
1

Published by John Wiley & Sons, Inc., Hoboken, New Jersey.
Published simultaneously in Canada.

For general information about our other products and services, please contact our Customer Care Department within the United States at (800) 762-2974, outside the United States at (317) 572-3993 or fax (317) 572-4002.

Wiley publishes in a variety of print and electronic formats and by print-on-demand. Some material included with standard print versions of this book may not be included in e-books or in print-on-demand. If this book refers to media such as a CD or DVD that is not included in the version you purchased, you may download this material at http://booksupport.wiley.com. For more information about Wiley products, visit www.wiley.com.

ISBN 9781119430261 (cloth); ISBN 9781119430506 (ePDF);
ISBN 9781119553267 (ePub)

Printed in the United States of America

R10003108_082218

THE HARD HAT

for Kids

A Story About
10 Ways to Be a
Great Teammate

JON GORDON and
LAUREN GALLAGHER, PhD

WILEY

Illustrated by **Korey Scott**

Mikayla loved three things in life:

Dogs,

triple chocolate ice cream cones,

and basketball.

Her grandfather was a coach, and Mikayla started playing basketball before she could even walk.

Mikayla, whom everyone called Mickey, played basketball all the time. She even begged her dad to put a light over the garage so she could play at night.

Mickey dreamed of the day fifth grade would begin and she could play basketball for her school team.

When the first day of fifth grade arrived, Mickey was ready. Well, she was ready for basketball at least.

The first day of school seemed to drag on forever. Finally Principal Rhodes's voice blared over the loudspeaker, "All fifth-graders interested in playing basketball, please report to the gym at dismissal!"

Mickey was out the door in a flash and halfway to the gym before Mr. Rhodes could finish his announcement.

"Welcome to Cayuga basketball!" said Coach Viola with a smile. "We kick off every season with the Hard Hat Award."
Mickey was instantly excited. She had been practicing every day and was ready for the chance to compete and win.

"This challenge is about being a great teammate. It will take place over the next week. After our first game, the winner will be awarded this big red hard hat." The kids looked at him excitedly, but they were a little puzzled.

Coach Viola chuckled. "I bet you're wondering why the prize is a hard hat. Well, a hard hat is usually worn by construction workers when they build tall buildings, bridges, and towers. Construction workers are known for working hard and working together to build something great."

"When I played lacrosse in college, my good friend George won our team's Hard Hat Award. He was the best teammate ever. To carry on this tradition, I will give this hard hat to the player who has been the best teammate throughout the next week."

Mickey was mesmerized by Coach Viola's story and she decided then and there that she wanted to win the hard hat.

Mickey knew she was the best basketball player on the team. She looked around and wondered if there was anyone who could give her some competition.

Her eyes fell on Jax and she smiled at him. He was the nicest kid at school and a pretty good player, but he couldn't make a basket or even get close to the rim.

During practice that week Mickey dribbled circles around everyone and made all her shots. The day before their first game, Jax said to Mickey, "You're a sharp shooter, Mickey! I hope I can learn to shoot like you one day!" Mickey was confident that the hard hat would be hers!

The next day, Mickey couldn't stop thinking about the game or the hard hat. Finally, it was time for the starting players to take the court.

The referee blew the whistle and Mickey's teammate Joe jumped and tipped the ball to her. She made a quick spin move, dribbled to the basket, and scored.

Mickey was a scoring machine! She already had 10 points when Coach Viola took her out. Mickey missed Jax's high-five because she was too busy stomping over to Coach Viola to complain.

"Coach, why did you take me out? I scored more points than anyone!"

"You were great out there, Mickey. Now it's time to be a great teammate from the bench," said Coach.

"How are you supposed to be a great teammate if you're not even in the game?" she mumbled to herself.

"Nice game today, and it was a great first week of practice! Now we have an award to give out," said Coach Viola, as he reached for the big, red, shiny hard hat. Mickey held her breath.

"After a lot of thought, I am excited to announce that the Hard Hat Award goes to Jax!

"Congratulations on winning the Hard Hat Award and for being such a great teammate."

As Mickey and her grandfather walked across the gym her grandfather said "Great game, Mickey! Why the sad face?"

"Pops, I was the best player on the team and I scored the most points, but I still didn't win the Hard Hat Award."

"Well, Mickey, there is a difference between being the best player and being the best teammate," said her grandfather.

"There is?" asked Mickey. "It sure is a mystery to me."

"Solving a mystery always begins with some good old-fashioned detective work and gathering clues," said her grandfather. "Why don't you start by watching Jax? Watch what he does at practice and during games. Even watch him when he's on the bench."

"Here you go. Every good detective needs a notebook for gathering clues," said her grandfather with a smile.

"Thanks, Pops!"

From that day on, Mickey imagined she was a detective. She watched Jax and searched for clues in the gym, on the court, during water breaks, on the bench, and even after practice. She put all the clues in her notebook.

After a week of detective work, she couldn't wait to share the clues with her grandfather that night at dinner.

1. Work
Hard

2. Effort

Mickey opened her notebook to show Pops her detective work. "I needed a way to make sense of all of these clues, so for each one I wrote a word or phrase to describe what Jax did. For example, he was always at the gym early to practice his shooting, so I used the words Work Hard and Effort.

"Even when our team was losing, Jax would cheer us on and shout out positive words that made us work harder and play better, so I used the words BELIEVE and ENCOURAGE.

"When Jax was on the bench, he watched his teammates play and always tried to motivate us. He made us believe we could win, so I used the words MOTIVATE and OPTIMISM.

"After every game Jax would shake the referee's hand and say, 'Thank you.'

"He also thanked Coach Viola after every game and practice, and always stayed after to help clean up the locker room, so I used the word

RESPECT.

"He huddled us up before every game and always shared positive energy.

"He never walked by a teammate without a smile and a high five and he was the first to jump off the bench with excitement when one of his teammates did something great on the court, so I used the words ENERGY and ENTHUSIASM.

"If you were having a bad practice or not playing well, Jax always said something helpful that made you feel better. He wasn't the best player but he made everyone around him better.

"He is a great friend so I wrote the word FRIEND."

"Wow, you've done a lot of work here, Mickey! So what do you make of it all?" asked her grandfather.

"Well, I felt all these words were the key to solving the mystery. When I put them in the right order, the answer was right there in front of me!"

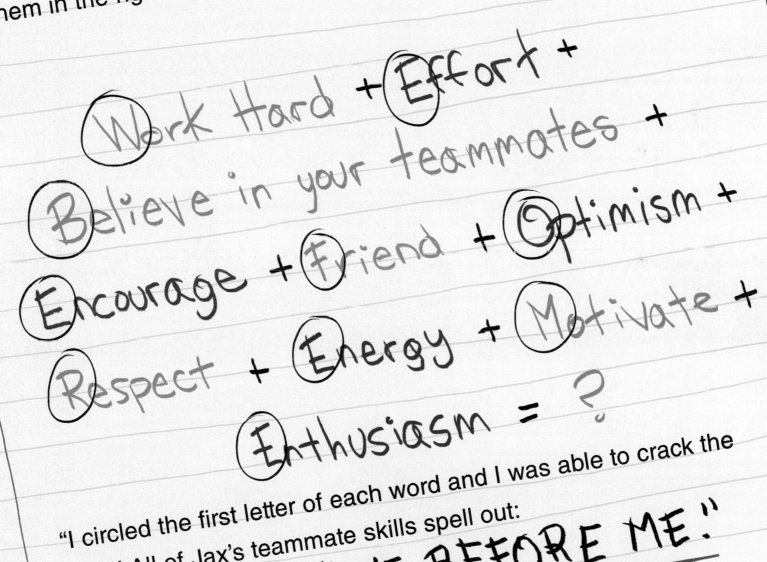

Work Hard + Effort +
Believe in your teammates +
Encourage + Friend + Optimism +
Respect + Energy + Motivate +
Enthusiasm = ?

"I circled the first letter of each word and I was able to crack the code! All of Jax's teammate skills spell out:

"WE BEFORE ME."

"You see, Pops? Jax always puts the team first and now that feeling is starting to spread!" said Mickey excitedly.

"What do you mean?" her grandfather asked.

"Jax once told me he wants to be able to shoot like me. Before, I only focused on being better than him, but now I want him to be the best he can be! He's shown us that we're all better when we put the team before ourselves."

"Well, my little detective, I think you've discovered the keys to being a great teammate," Mickey's grandfather said with a smile.

From that day forward, Mickey and Jax met every day to practice their shooting. Mickey taught him all the shooting tips she had learned from her grandfather.

One day after cleaning up the locker room, they walked home together.

"I can't believe the championship game is tomorrow," said Jax. "Coach says we have a good shot at beating the Lions."

"With your new shooting skills the Lions have no chance!" said Mickey as she smiled and headed home.

The next day, the whole school came to watch Cayuga play in the championship. As time ticked away, Cayuga was still down by a point when Coach Viola called a time-out. "We have time for one last play. Let's go with Big Red, the play where Ezra passes the ball to Mickey for the shot."

Mickey had waited for this moment her whole life. It was her chance to make the winning shot in a championship game. She looked over at Jax and suddenly had a different idea.

"Coach, I have two players on me and I don't think I'll be able to get a shot off. What if I fake the shot and pass it to Jax?" she asked hopefully.

Coach Viola looked surprised, then smiled. "Great idea Mickey! Jax, get ready!"

The whistle blew and Ezra passed the ball to Mickey, who instantly had two players on her. She quickly faked the shot, causing the defenders to jump in the air.

She then delivered a perfect bounce pass between them to Jax, who was ready and waiting.

Jax caught the ball. He looked at Mickey. She nodded. The gym was silent.

Jax bent his legs, just like he and Mickey had practiced, and then jumped and released the ball toward the basket.

Time seemed to stand still as all eyes followed the ball through the air. SWISH! The buzzer sounded! The whole gym erupted with cheers! Cayuga Elementary had won the championship!

After the game, Coach Viola called the team to the locker room one last time. "I'm so proud of all of you for making this such a great season! You really came together as a team and showed what the hard hat is all about. And congrats to our Hard Hat winner, Jax, for a fearless winning basket."

Jax then stood up and said, "Thank you, Coach, but there's someone who deserves the hard hat more than me."

Jax walked over to Mickey and put the hard hat on her head. "You helped me become a better shooter. You passed me the ball. You encouraged me. You are not only a great player, but you are also a great teammate and you deserve the hard hat." The team cheered and clapped as Mickey smiled.

In that moment, Mickey realized that the hard hat itself wasn't important. Being a great teammate and making your team better was what mattered most.

She discovered that being a great teammate means that sometimes you are the star, and other times you help your teammate become the star.

When Coach Viola went into the locker room the next day, he found the hard hat sitting in its place on the shelf and a message taped above it.

Dear Coach,

We decided to leave the hard hat here for the next team, along with the 10 important ways to be a great teammate. Just as your teammate George inspired you, we want to inspire people as well.

Thanks for everything, Coach,

Mickey & Jax   "WE BEFORE ME"

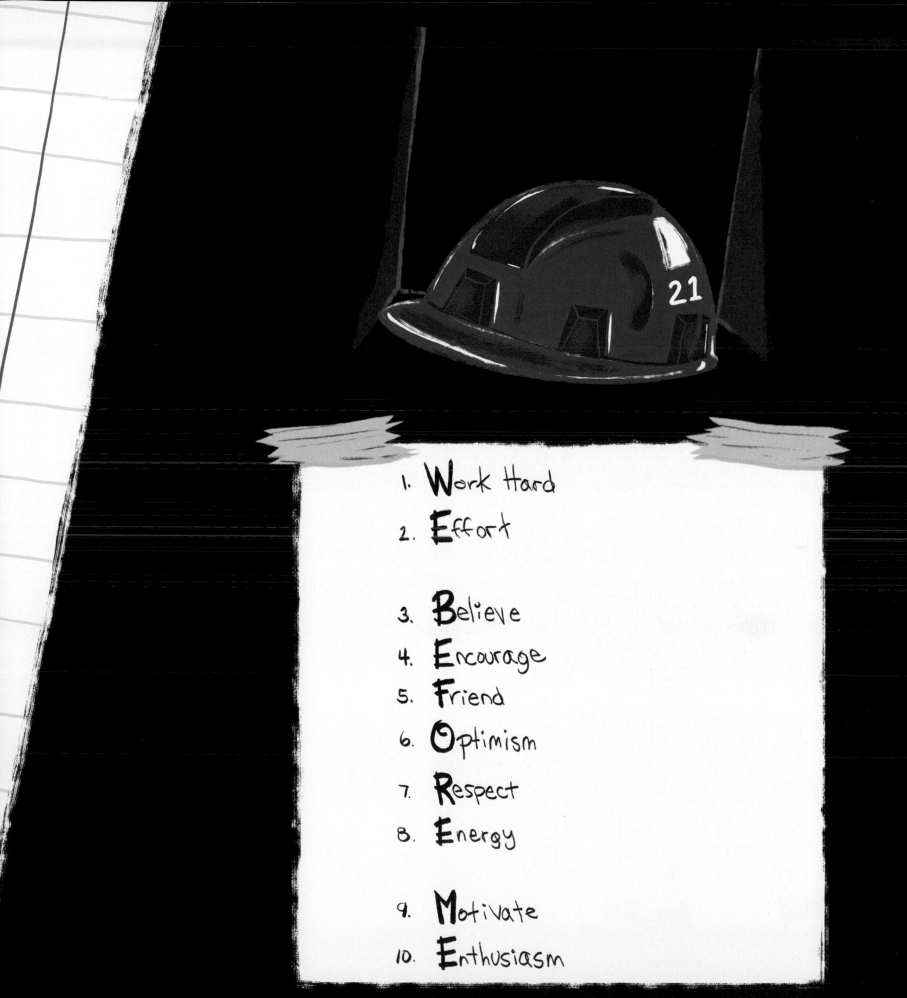

Complimentary Resources

Visit www.HardHatKids.com for a free Discussion Guide and Activity Guide for teachers and parents.

Utilize in the classroom or at home to reinforce the principles and lessons found in this book.

Bring the Hard Hat to Your School

Jon Gordon is passionate about developing positive schools, educators, and kids. He and his team of positive teachers have worked with countless school districts that have utilized The Hard Hat principles to enhance morale, improve teacher performance, and inspire students.

Programs include:

- Hard Hat Retreats for Principals
- Hard Hat Workshops for Teachers
- Readings in the Classroom with Illustrator Korey Scott
- Student Assemblies

For more information contact The Jon Gordon Companies at:

Phone: (904) 285-6842

Email: info@jongordon.com

Website: www.HardHatKids.com

Facebook.com/JonGordonPage

Twitter: @JonGordon11

Other Children's Books by Jon Gordon

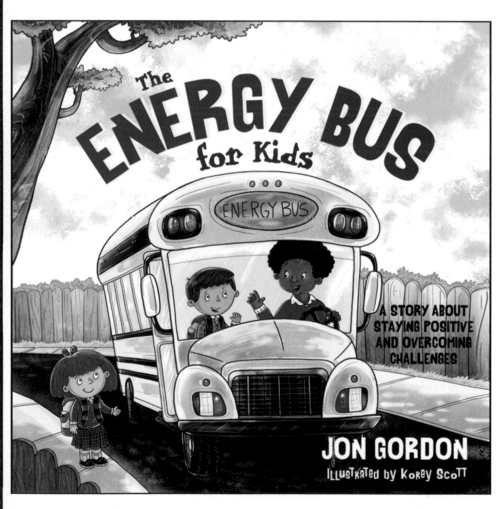

The Energy Bus for Kids

The illustrated children's adaptation of the bestselling book *The Energy Bus* tells the story of George, who, with the help of his school bus driver, Joy, learns that if he believes in himself, he'll find the strength to overcome any challenge. His journey teaches kids how to overcome negativity, bullies, and everyday challenges to be their best.

www.EnergyBusKids.com

Thank You and Good Night

Thank You and Good Night is a beautifully illustrated book that shares the heart of gratitude. Jon Gordon takes a little boy and girl on a fun-filled journey from one perfect moonlit night to the next. During their adventurous days and nights, the children explore the people, places, and things that they are thankful for.

The two tots in *Thank You and Good Night* learn that being thankful makes ice cream taste better, butterflies look more beautiful, and weekend days seem longer. "Thank you" is a phrase that will brighten any kid's day and help them get a good night's sleep.